Start Small, Grow Big: A Blueprint for Business Growth

Kingsley Eleweke

DISCLAIMER

Start Small, Grow Big: A Blueprint for Business Growth

Kingsley Eleweke © **2024– All Rights Reserved**

No part of this book may be reproduced, stored, or transmitted in any form or by any means, including mechanical or electronic, without prior written permission from the author.

While the author has made every effort to ensure that the ideas, statistics, and the information presented in this book are accurate to the best of his/her abilities, any implications direct, derived, or perceived, should only be used at the reader's discretion.

The author cannot be held responsible for any personal or commercial damage arising from communication, application, or misinterpretation of the information presented herein.

All Rights Reserved.

Website: www.toptoria.com

TABLE OF CONTENTS

INTRODUCTION

Warren Buffet once said, "The difference between successful people and very successful people is that very successful people say no to almost everything." It's a profound statement, isn't it? It emphasizes the importance of focus and strategic decision-making in achieving significant success.

Now, when it comes to running a successful business, it requires efficient allocation of resources and prioritization of tasks. Not just about ramping up leads and sales. Sure, those are vital for keeping your business afloat, but they might not be enough to achieve all your lofty business goals.

To truly take your business to new heights, you've got to have a solid plan and stick to it. So, if you're serious about growing your business, you can't rely on vague, scattered ideas. What you need is a well-thought-out growth strategy. With a clear roadmap in hand, you'll have a much better grasp of where your business is headed and how to get there.

Expanding your business is an exhilarating prospect. It means you're already delivering value to your customers and making them happy.
But let's not sugarcoat it – it's also a time fraught with challenges and risks. That's why it's crucial to develop a comprehensive plan that helps you navigate through uncertainties with confidence.

But before you dive into drafting that business plan, it's essential to take a good, hard look at where you stand right now. Understanding your current situation inside out will empower you to identify areas for improvement and innovation that can propel your business forward.

Whether you're a seasoned entrepreneur or just starting out, by the end of this book, "Start Small, Grow Big: A Blueprint for Business Growth," armed with your newfound insights, you'll be well-equipped to lay a solid foundation and empowered to make informed decisions about the future direction of your business. Remember, it all starts with taking small steps towards your big goals.

CHAPTER 1: A SIMPLE IDEA

Every successful business starts with an owner who has a vision for making money. Although these concepts are often simple, turning them into reality demands months of unwavering dedication and hard work. These visionary individuals, propelled by their determination, saw their ideas through and ultimately crafted thriving enterprises.

Similarly, this book is a product of entrepreneurial spirit, stemming from an idea much like those behind the businesses we encounter daily. Just as with any successful venture, your next job or income stream could stem from a basic idea and blossom from there.

No business emerges fully formed; they all start as seeds of inspiration. Whether your business concept involves producing goods or providing services, , the ultimate aim remains the same: turning a profit. However, to achieve profitability in any chosen line of business, your goods or services must meet the needs of your target audience.

Choosing to start your own business is a significant, life-altering decision that will impact you for years to come. There are no guarantees, and undoubtedly, you will encounter numerous hurdles along the way. Nonetheless, certain keys can unlock your path to success, and it is these keys that we will explore in this book.

My Business Genesis

You might be wondering, "What business experience do you bring to the table?" Well, allow me to take you on a journey that began several years ago while I pursued my M.Sc. in Economics. This journey has led me to unexpected places, catapulting my products and services into the hands of countless loyal customers worldwide, with sales spanning across major countries.

I am confident you'll find value in what I offer because my background includes hands-on experience in running a real-world business, selling tangible products, and delivering services to a global audience. I'm eager to share invaluable business insights that I believe will fuel the growth of your small business.

Embarking on a business venture from scratch, especially with limited funds, can seem scary. I started just like many small business owners, armed with nothing but a vision and determination. Despite the financial constraints, I remained resolute in my desire to realize my dreams.

While staying in my university hostel, I provided statistical data analysis and research services. It was then that I realized the potential of entrepreneurship based on services as a way to generate income from scratch.

In today's fast-paced world, where time is a precious commodity, there remains a significant demand for service-oriented businesses. In the beginning, my driving force was clear: to build a profitable venture that would grant me financial freedom.

I must also emphasize that dedication and a willingness to go the extra mile have been pivotal in my efforts to build a sustainable business. I have made personal sacrifices to ensure that my endeavor succeeds, fueled by a relentless commitment to reaching new heights.

Guiding Mantras for Entrepreneurs

Every business owner encounters various challenges along the way, but rest assured, you can overcome these challenges. Your reasons for starting a business could be diverse. Some may have been drawn by the potential financial gains, while others sought the flexibility it offers in managing their time.

Whatever your motivation, I believe you made informed decisions before embarking on this journey, aiming for both beneficial and successful outcomes. For those aspiring to start their own business, it's advisable to first identify a business opportunity and then gather the necessary resources and market insights before launching.

Success as a new startup hinges on addressing key issues during the planning stage. In my experience, when I started out, I focused on understanding the motivation behind my decision to start a business. Despite facing challenges, what kept me going was my perseverance and motivation.

Motivation plays a pivotal role in determining the success of your business. Your personal commitment and passion for your chosen venture are crucial for its success.

As society evolves, innovative entrepreneurs identify new needs and desires and provide solutions that are both profitable and beneficial to society.

When there is demand for a product or service, it presents an opportunity to start a business. However, many individuals and startups struggle to take off. Here are some guiding mantras to follow:

- Action Attracts Action

Even if your business plan isn't perfect initially, don't let that hinder you from launching. Perfection is elusive; instead, focus on refining and adapting as you progress.

- Be Open to New Ideas

Remain receptive to new techniques, programs, or ideas that could benefit your business. Flexibility is key to growth.

- Research Your Competitors

Understanding your competitors and their strategies is essential for shaping your own approach and fostering growth.

Starting a business can be immensely fulfilling but also demanding. It requires dedication, discipline, and self-motivation. It's crucial to assess your life, personality, and work ethic realistically to determine if you're up for the challenge.

Despite the challenges, becoming your own boss can lead to incredible experiences and personal growth. You can follow in the footsteps of successful entrepreneurs by carefully observing your environment and identifying unmet needs.

Entrepreneurs are adept at turning problems into opportunities and creating new industries. Their mindset revolves around job creation rather than job seeking, and they thrive on solving problems. Ultimately, entrepreneurs are catalysts for positive change in society, creating jobs, and offering hope to many.

CHAPTER 2: BUSINESS STRUCTURES UNVEILED

As you prepare to enter the business world, it's important to consider some essential steps you must take beforehand. Your goal should be more than just creating products, serving customers, or making money; it's about building a business that can thrive and survive over time.

While it might seem as easy as pie to start selling your goods and services around town, there are regulations governing how we conduct businesses. One essential step before launching your business is ensuring its legal status.

You'll need to select a legal structure for your business. Though it may feel overwhelming to sift through all the necessary information, however, laying this groundwork initially, will pave the way for your long-term success.

From a legal standpoint, your business could take the form of a sole proprietorship, a partnership, or a corporation. Each structure comes with its own set of advantages and disadvantages, and your choice should align with your available capital and preferences.

The Sole Proprietorship

In a sole proprietorship, a single individual owns the business-known as the proprietor – he/she reaps all the profits and bears all the debts. Compared to other business structures, this setup is the simplest to establish and is commonly favored by small businesses with minimal personal liability concerns.

The benefits of this arrangement include the ease of setup, the autonomy it affords the owner in decision-making and unrestricted access to business profits. However, there are downsides to sole proprietorship, with the most significant being the proprietor's unlimited liability.

As a sole business owner, you're personally liable for all business debts, leaving your personal assets vulnerable to creditors' claims. One of the challenges faced by single-owner businesses is securing capital and retaining key employees. These businesses often have limited resources and opportunities for employee advancement.

The Partnership Route

A partnership involves two or more individuals pooling their resources to establish a business. Partners jointly own, control, manage, and share in the business's profits and losses.

Similar to sole proprietorship, partnerships are straightforward to set up with minimal paperwork. The key advantages of partnerships over sole proprietorships include access to a broader range of skills and resources, increased capital availability, and the potential for employees to become partners.

When forming a partnership, it's advisable to document each partner's obligations, investments, and profit shares through a partnership agreement. However, partnerships share the same drawback as sole proprietorships regarding unlimited liability, but to a greater extent.

In a partnership, partners are not only liable for their own debts but also those incurred by their partners. This exposes partners to potential legal and financial risks, including disputes among partners that could hinder business growth unless addressed through a predefined dispute resolution process.
Experts generally advise against partnerships due to the lack of personal liability protection for general partners, which can lead to legal and interpersonal conflicts.

The Corporate Choice

When considering business structures, it's important to understand the options available to you. Unlike sole proprietorships or partnerships, corporations offer greater flexibility and autonomy.

Legally, a corporation is treated as a separate entity, much like an individual person. This distinction means that it operates independently from its owners, granting it the ability to engage in various commercial activities such as owning property, entering into contracts, and pursuing legal actions.

One significant advantage of a corporation is limited liability for its owners, known as shareholders. This means that shareholders are only liable for the amount of capital they've invested in the company, safeguarding their personal assets.

Additionally, corporations enjoy benefits such as easier access to capital, a larger pool of human resources, and enhanced credibility in the eyes of potential clients. However, it's crucial to consider the drawbacks as well. Corporations face taxation on both corporate income and individual shareholder income, leading to potential complexities and higher expenses.

Moreover, setting up a corporation involves more intricate legal and financial processes compared to sole proprietorships or partnerships.
Given your starting budget constraints, we recommend starting as a sole proprietorship unless you have sufficient capital to launch a larger-scale operation.

This option offers simplicity and affordability, making it an ideal choice for entrepreneurs beginning their journey. Understanding the nuances of each business structure is vital to making informed decisions that aligns with your goals and resources.

Whether you opt for a sole proprietorship, partnership, or corporation, each has its own set of advantages and considerations to weigh.

CHAPTER 3: SECRET INGREDIENTS OF SUCCESSFUL ENTREPRENEURS

Entrepreneurs are everywhere, embodying independence and determination as they forge ahead with their own ventures. Embarking on the journey of starting a business can feel daunting at first and questions flood the mind:

➤ What business should I pursue?
➤ Where will the necessary funds come from?
➤ How do I attract customers?

These concerns are valid, yet each one can be addressed systematically. Consider this: as you navigate through the city streets, nearly every establishment you pass is a testament to someone who once stood in your shoes, grappling with the same uncertainties.

Yet, they persevered, learned the ropes, secured funding, and built a customer base. If they could do it, so can you. The secret is in diligent preparation. Entrepreneurs embody optimism, constantly chasing success while embracing failure as a stepping stone to growth.

However, they possess distinct qualities and skills that set them apart. If you're an aspiring entrepreneur or business owner, you know that success isn't easy. But what if you could learn from the experiences of those who have achieved great success?

In our exploration, we'll delve into entrepreneur personality self-assessment test so that you can gain a comprehensive understanding of what makes entrepreneurs tick, empowering you to launch your own successful venture.

Personality Traits of Winning Entrepreneurs

Whether you're an entrepreneur or you own a business, your success goes beyond just having a brilliant idea. It will demand your dedication, focus, and willingness—a blend of passion and perseverance—to achieve unique, long-term goals.

Here are habits of highly successful people that you can adopt to propel yourself towards building a lasting endeavor:

- **Set Firm Deadlines**: Have an ambitious goal that you are aiming at and establish a deadline to keep yourself accountable and motivated towards achieving it.. For instance, you can set an ambitious target for your product production or launch. You can strive to release a product with unwavering regularity, akin to precision, which will keep you on course and lead to success.
- **Maintain Laser Focus**: Dedicate your full attention to a single project. Concentrating on a single project with pinpoint precision will help you to see through to its completion, without getting distracted by other enticing opportunities.
- **Prioritize Progress over Perfection**: Prioritize getting your good product out as quickly as possible, rather than chasing perfection. Start with a minimum viable product (MVP) if necessary. Perfection is often difficult to attain, iterate and

improve over time,

- **Embrace Challenges**: Winners welcome challenges and persist in the face of failure. They view mistakes as opportunities for growth and learning.
- **Actively Seek Mistakes:** Always actively, seek out your mistakes and learn from them to avoid repeating them in the future. Identifying areas you need to improve will help you to achieve long term success.
- **Commit to Lifelong Learning**: Be a perpetual learner. Humbly acknowledge that you don't have all the answers. Actively seek knowledge and advice from various sources, including successful peers and timeless principles.
- **Focus on Unique Value**: Pay attention to your unique selling proposition (USP) rather than trying to cater to everyone. Your USP sets you apart and will help you to stand out in a crowded market.
- **Capitalize on Strengths and Delegate Weaknesses**: Identify your strengths and focus on improving them, while you delegate tasks that fall outside your expertise. There is value in collaboration and teamwork.
- **Surround Yourself with Growth**: Have mentors, attend conferences, and build relationships with people who will challenge you to grow. Supportive network will enable you to navigate the challenges of entrepreneurship.
- **Prioritize Marketing:** Marketing is very important. Invest in strategies to promote your products or services effectively. Employ various channels, from social media to traditional advertising, to reach your target audience.
- **Stay Focused and Disciplined**: Remain steadfast in your pursuit of goals. Manage your time efficiently and eliminate all distractions along the way.

While success is not a one-size-fits-all formula, adopting these habits can undoubtedly set you on the path to success.

Personality Traits of Losing Entrepreneurs

Now, let's address the challenges some face in the entrepreneurial journey. It's natural to encounter stumbling blocks along the way; failure is an inherent aspect of this journey.

Until you confront your fears and view failure as a chance to learn, you may find yourself stagnating. Let's examine some characteristics of individuals who consistently struggle and see if any resonate with you:

- **Lack of Focus and Accountability:** These individuals struggle to adhere to deadlines or targets. They find it difficult to maintain focus, resulting in missed opportunities and unmet goals.
- **Succumbing to Distractions:** They're easily enticed by new opportunities and find it hard to commit fully to any one project. This fear of missing out leads them to juggle multiple ventures but excel in none.
- **Pursuit of Perfection**: They delay launching their product in pursuit of perfection, fearing failure. However, this reluctance to take risks prevents them from learning and growing through experience.
- **Fear of Failure**: They're paralyzed by the fear of failure, hindering their ability to take risks or overcome obstacles. Rather than facing challenges head-on, they retreat or shift blame when things don't go as planned.

- **Refusal to Acknowledge Mistakes:** They resist acknowledging their mistakes and instead blame others for their shortcomings. This refusal to accept responsibility hinders personal and professional development.
- **Envy of Others' Success:** They view successful individuals with envy, making excuses for their own lack of progress. Instead of emulating success, they dwell on perceived differences as justification for their failures.
- **Lack of Originality:** They forsake their unique selling points and attempt to imitate others, often with inferior results, undermines their ability to stand out in the market.
- **Reluctance to Delegate:** They insist on handling everything themselves, believing they're the only ones capable. However, this refusal to delegate leads to burnout and subpar outcomes.
- **Avoidance of Successful Mentors:** They're too proud to seek guidance from those who've achieved success, missing out on valuable insights and mentorship opportunities.
- **Greed:** They prioritize personal gain over collaboration and sharing success with others. This shortsightedness limits potential partnerships and growth opportunities.
- **Neglect of Marketing:** They focus solely on product development, neglecting the importance of effective marketing. Without a solid marketing strategy, even the best product may go unnoticed.
- Proclivity for Distraction: They welcome distractions as a means of avoiding confronting their challenges. These distractions hinder progress toward their goals.

The common pitfalls that can impede progress in your business can be overcome by pivoting towards your aspirations. Success isn't merely about possessing a stellar product; it's equally about cultivating the right mindset and embarking on decisive action. It hinges on focus, discipline, a willingness to venture into the unknown, and the humility to learn from missteps.

Entrepreneur Personality Self-Assessment Test

This entrepreneur personality self-assessment test is designed to illuminate your strengths, passions, and potential in the world of business. This is not just any test, it is a compass that guides you towards a better understanding of yourself and your entrepreneurial aspirations.

So, please be honest as you navigate through it because only through honesty can you uncover the insights required for meaningful growth.

1. **Are you a self-starter?**
    a. Yes, I like to think up ideas and implement them. (5 points)
    b. **If someone helps me get started, I will definitely follow through. (3 points)**
    c. **Frankly, I would rather follow than lead. (1 point)**
2. **How do you feel about taking risks?**
    a. I really like the feeling of being on the edge a bit. (5 points)
    b. **Calculated risks are acceptable at times. (3 points)**
    c. **I like the tried and true. (1 point)**
3. **Are you a leader?**
    a. Yes. (5 points)
    b. **Yes, when necessary. (3 points)**
    c. **No, not really. (1 point)**
4. **Can you and your family live without a regular paycheck?**
    a. Yes, if that is what it takes. (5 points)
    b. **I would rather not, but understand that may be part of the process. (3 points)**

      c. **I do not like that idea at all. (1 point)**

5. **Could you fire someone who really needed the job your business provided?**
   a. Yes. I may not like it, but that is the way it goes sometimes. (5 points)
   b. **I hope so. (3 points)**
   c. **I really can't see myself doing that. (1 point)**

6. **Are you willing to work 60 hours a week, or more?**
   a. Again, if that is what it takes, yes. (5 points)
   b. **Maybe in the beginning. (3 points)**
   c. **I think many other things are more important than work.(1 point)**

7. **Are you self-confident?**
   a. You bet! (5 points)
   b. **Most of the time. (3 points)**
   c. **Unfortunately, that is not one of my strong suits. (1 point)**

8. **Can you live with uncertainty?**
   a. Yes. (5 points)
   b. **If I have to, but I don't like it. (3 points)**
   c. **No, I like knowing what to expect. (1 point)**

9. **Can you stick with it once you have put your mind to something?**
   a. I usually will not let anything get in the way. (5 points)
   b. **Most of the time, if I like what I am doing. (3 points)**
   c. **Not always. (1 point)**

10. **Are you creative?**
    a. Yes, I do get a lot of good ideas. (5 points)
    b. **I can be. (3 points)**
    c. **No, not really. (1 point)**

11. **Are you competitive?**
    a. To a fault sometimes. (5 points)
    b. **Sure, mostly. (3 points)**
    c. **Not really, my nature is more laid-back. (1 point)**

12. Do you have a lot of willpower and self-discipline?
    a. Yes. (5 points)
    b. I am self-disciplined when I need to be. (3 points)
    c. Not really. (1 point)

13. **Are you individualistic or would you rather go along with the status quo?**
    a. I like to think things through myself and do things my way. (5 points)
    b. **I am sometimes an original. (3 points)**
    c. **I think strongly individualistic people are a bit strange. (1 point)**
14. **Can you live without structure?**
    a. Yes. (5 points)
    b. **Actually, the idea of living without a regular job makes me nervous. (3 points)**
    c. **No, I like routine and structure in my life. (1 point)**
15. **Do you have many business skills?**
    a. Yes, I do, and those I don't have, I'll learn. (5 points)
    b. **I have some. (3 points)**
    c. **No, not really. (1 point)**
16. **Are you flexible and willing to change course when things are not** going your way?
    a. Yes. (5 points)
    b. I like to think so, but others may disagree. (3 points)
    c. No, I have a fairly rigid personality. (1 point)
17. **Do you have experience in the business you are thinking of starting?**
    a. Yes. (5 points)
    b. **Some. (3 points)**
    c. **No. (1 point)**
18. **Could you competently perform multiple business tasks: accounting, sales, marketing, and so on?**
    a. I sure would like to try! (5 points)
    b. **I hope so. (3 points)**
    c. **That sounds intimidating. (1 point)**
19. **Are you willing to really hustle for clients and customers?**
    a. Sure. (5 points)
    b. **If I have to. (3 points)**
    c. **I would rather not. (1 point)**
20. **How well do you handle pressure?**
    a. Quite well. (5 points)

    b. It's not my strongest trait, but I can do it. (3 points)

    c. Not well at all. (1 point)

Scoring

If your score falls between 80 and 100, congratulations! You possess both the temperament and the skills necessary to thrive as an entrepreneur.

For scores ranging from 60 to 79, while you may not inherently possess all the qualities of a natural entrepreneur, with time and dedication, you have the potential to develop into one.

If your score is below 60, it might be prudent to consider exploring alternative career paths instead of pursuing self-employment.

This quiz serves not only to assess your Entrepreneurship IQ but also to offer valuable insights into the traits and characteristics commonly found in successful self-employed individuals: drive, hard work, creativity, energy, resourcefulness, confidence, and adaptability.

If these qualities resonate with you (or come close), then the next question beckons: where do you go from here?

CHAPTER 4: BUSINESS ENVIRONMENTS

In economics, a business thrives within its surroundings and forges a symbiotic relationship with its environment. Its journey from survival to growth hinges upon the conditions it encounters.

These conditions, collectively known as the business environment, encompass a myriad of factors that directly or indirectly influence its trajectory. Social, political, legal, economic, technological, geographical, and demographic elements intertwine to shape this dynamic landscape.

Indeed, a business finds its opportunities within this environment, yet its ability to adapt is paramount. Failure to synchronize with its surroundings can lead to downfall.

Therefore, the concept of the business environment encompasses all the direct and indirect components that mold a business's activities.
For every entrepreneur, navigating the ever-evolving business environment is a constant endeavor. As a business owner, your enterprise is inherently intertwined with the environment it inhabits.

These environmental conditions, or forces, present both challenges and opportunities. Success lies in your ability to discern these factors and mitigate their impact, especially the unfavorable ones. To comprehend the interplay between environments and businesses, one must scrutinize current scenarios and developments.

Each business is uniquely affected by its environment, making it imperative to assess potential changes' ramifications. This understanding equips you with the knowledge to:

> Anticipate the demands your environment will place on your business.
> Identify the constraints it may impose.
> Capitalize on the opportunities it presents for your success.
> Safeguard against potential threats, either by neutralizing or circumventing them.

The business environment can be categorized into two main types:

1. **Internal:** The internal environment pertains to factors within your control
2. **External:** The external environment comprises external influences beyond your immediate reach.

Change is the one constant in life. It's inevitable, and for organizations, embracing change and adapting their business models accordingly is paramount for success.

Understanding Your Organization's Internal Environment

Your business's internal environment consists of factors that lie within the control of your organization. These elements can either bolster or challenge your organization's strengths and weaknesses.

As an entrepreneur or business owner, it falls upon you to ensure the survival and success of your business. You can achieve this by forecasting and adapting to changes within your business environment, thereby unlocking new opportunities and fostering growth.

In navigating the internal workings of your organization, it's crucial to grasp the various elements that compose its environment. These elements serve as the foundation for your business's operations and growth. Let's delve into each one:

1. **Business Goals**

At the heart of your organization lie its aspirations – the business goals. These are the milestones you aim to achieve in the future. Whether it's boosting profits, expanding your market reach, or fulfilling social responsibilities, your business activities are all geared towards realizing these objectives.

2. **Business Policies**

Think of policies as guiding stars illuminating the path for every facet of your organization. They provide the overarching principles that steer activities across departments, ensuring harmony and alignment towards common objectives.

3. **Business Resources**

Your organization's arsenal for success comprises various resources, both tangible and intangible. Tangible resources include capital, equipment, and raw materials, while intangible ones encompass knowledge, skills, and innovation capacity. These resources aren't just tools; they're the fuel propelling your organization forward, offering a competitive edge in the dynamic market landscape.

> **Tangible Resources**
>   - **Financial Resources:** Your organization's financial prowess, crucial for sustaining operations.
>   - **Organizational Resources:** The backbone of your

operations, encompassing information, structure, and control mechanisms.

- **Physical Resources:** From machinery to raw materials, these tangible assets drive your production processes.

➢ **Intangible Resources**

- **Human Resources:** The collective expertise, skills, and leadership qualities of your team.
- **Innovation Resources:** The ability to think outside the box and drive progress through creativity and strategic innovation.
- **Reputational Resources:** Building trust and loyalty through exceptional customer relationships and consistent quality.

4. Organizational Structure

Picture your organization as a well-oiled machine, with each component – roles, responsibilities, and relationships – intricately defined by its structure. Clarity in this framework is paramount, ensuring smooth execution of strategies and swift adaptation to evolving challenges.

5. Organizational Culture

Beyond mere policies and structures lies the soul of your organization – its culture. This encompasses shared values, norms, and behaviors that define how your organization operates. It's the invisible force shaping decisions, interactions, and the overall vibe within your workplace.

In essence, understanding and nurturing these elements of your organization's internal environment pave the way for sustainable growth and success. They form the bedrock upon which your business thrives, evolves, and makes a meaningful impact in the ever-changing business landscape.

Understanding the External Environment of an Organization

The external environment of a business comprises factors outside the organization's control that influence its operations, performance, and strategic decisions. It includes various elements in the broader business environment that impact the organization. Key components of the external environment include:

- **Economic Factors:** Conditions such as economic growth, inflation, interest rates, exchange rates, and consumer spending patterns.
- **Social and Cultural Factors:** Demographics, cultural trends, values, lifestyles, consumer preferences, and societal norms.
- **Technological Factors:** Advancements, innovations, digitalization, automation, and technological disruptions that affect industries and markets.
- **Legal and Regulatory Factors:** Laws, regulations, government policies, and compliance requirements related to labor, taxation, environmental protection, consumer protection, and industry standards.
- **Political Factors:** Government stability, political ideologies, policies, trade relations, geopolitical tensions, and political risks.
- **Competitive Factors:** The competitive landscape, industry rivalry, competitors' strategies, market share, pricing dynamics, and barriers to entry.
- **Global Factors:** International trade agreements, geopolitical events, global market trends, cultural differences, and opportunities and risks associated with globalization.

In navigating the external environment, we encounter two significant domains: the General Environment and the Task Environment.

1. The General Environment

The General Environment consists of broad, macro-level factors that affect all organizations within a specific industry or market. Although individual businesses may not have direct control over these factors, their impact on operations and strategic decisions is significant. This environment includes:

> **Economic Environment:** At the heart of the General Environment lies the Economic Environment, which shapes the economic landscape in which a firm operates. It dictates the costs of essential inputs and influences consumer purchasing power. Key components of the Economic Environment include:

- **Economic Systems:** These systems, including the Free Market Economy, Centrally Planned Economy, and Mixed System, define the extent of private and public sector involvement in the economy.
- **Economic Policies:** Governmental guidelines, such as Monetary, Fiscal, and Industrial policies, aim to foster economic development and regulate economic activities.
- **Economic Conditions:** Indicators like Gross Domestic Product (GDP), inflation rates, employment statistics, balance of payments, and income distribution offer insights into the economic health of a nation.
- **Business Cycles:** The fluctuating phases of depression, recovery, prosperity, and recession profoundly impact organizational well-being.
- **Economic Integration:** Regional and global economic integration initiatives facilitate free trade and cooperation among nations, influencing market dynamics.

> **Political and Legal Environment:** Laws and governmental

actions serve as the regulatory framework within which businesses operate. These factors not only set the parameters for business conduct but also impact managerial decisions and long-term planning.

➤ **Technological Factors:** Technological advancements, innovations, breakthroughs, digitalization trends, and the rate of technological change impact industries, products, services, and business processes.

➤ **Socio-Cultural Environment:** Embedded within society, businesses must navigate the intricate web of cultural and social norms that shape consumer behavior and preferences. This environment encompasses:
  - **Consumer Behavior:** Consumers' norms, beliefs, attitudes, and language influence their interactions with products and organizations, necessitating businesses to tailor their strategies accordingly.

In essence, the General Environment represents a tapestry of economic, political, legal, and socio-cultural factors that exert a profound influence on organizational dynamics. Understanding and adeptly navigating these elements are essential for business success in today's interconnected world.

2. Task Environment

The Task Environment plays a crucial role in an organization's journey toward achieving its goals. This environment encompasses various factors that directly impact the organization's ability to succeed. Think of it as the backdrop against which the company operates and strives to thrive.

So, what exactly is this Task Environment?

Simply put, it consists of the conditions stemming from suppliers, distributors, customers, stock markets, and competitors. These elements are like pieces of a puzzle, each contributing to the overall picture of the organization's challenges and opportunities.

Understanding the Task Environment is key for any business. It's like having a compass that guides decision-making and strategy development. By recognizing the factors within this environment, a company gains valuable insights into what drives its success.

Suppliers, distributors, customers, stock markets, and competitors—all play vital roles in shaping the Task Environment. They're not just external entities; they're partners, influencers, and sometimes even competitors themselves. Their actions and dynamics directly impact how a company operates and evolves.
In essence, the Task Environment is about understanding the landscape in which a business operates. It's about acknowledging the interconnectedness of various elements and leveraging this understanding to navigate toward success.

By embracing this holistic view, organizations can better position themselves to thrive amidst the ever-changing dynamics of the business world. The task environment includes:

- **Customers:** Customers are the most critical component of the task environment. All business activities are aimed at satisfying customer needs and effectively retaining them. Customers may be individuals, families, or businesses. In addition to purchasing goods and services, they also serve as sources of information and ideas. Strategic management should consistently focus on addressing the evolving needs and demands of customers and fostering long-term relationships with them.
- **Suppliers**: Suppliers are individuals or firms that provide inputs to businesses needed to produce goods and services. The quality of the product depends on the quality of inputs. In addition to quality, factors

such as price, delivery time, and terms and conditions are also crucial for a business. A strong relationship with suppliers always presents opportunities for the business.

- **Competitors**: Competitors are firms that offer similar products in the same market. Businesses compete for customers, necessitating a thorough analysis of competitors through competitive intelligence, where firms gather data and information to understand competitors' objectives, strategies, assumptions, and capabilities. Competition occurs within strategic groups, which are sets of firms emphasizing similar strategic dimensions and employing similar strategies. Therefore, the activities of key competitors within the same strategic group are crucial for a business.
- **Distributors**: Distribution management is a critical factor that determines a business's effectiveness. A robust distribution system enables a business to deliver products and services to consumers within a stipulated time. Distributors also provide significant support to the supplier or manufacturer's promotional efforts in terms of manpower and financial resources. Therefore, it is essential for a business to maintain close relationships with distributors.
- **Media:** Businesses are closely intertwined with the media, as the media closely monitors business activities and significantly influences a business's image. Continuous interaction with the media can create numerous opportunities for a business, making it necessary to address media inquiries promptly.
- **Regulators**: Government agencies, regulatory bodies, industry associations, and other authorities that oversee and regulate the activities of the organization and its industry.
- Partnerships and Alliances: Collaborative relationships, strategic alliances, joint ventures, and

partnerships formed with other organizations to achieve common goals or pursue mutual interests.

An organization must have the ability to examine and make changes based on internal and external environmental factors that affect its performance. The use of appropriate business tools to analyze these environmental factors is critical to the success of an organization.

CHAPTER 5: DISCOVERING POTENTIAL BUSINESS OPPORTUNITIES

Discovering potential business opportunities isn't the challenge; they're everywhere. However, often we blame the lack of opportunity for our financial struggles when, in reality, the issue lies within ourselves. You may want to ask:

"How do I raise money to start my own business?"

My response is: "What business idea do you have?"

I emphasize that; above all else, a solid business idea is paramount. Identifying a promising opportunity will enable you to build a successful venture. It's crucial not to dive into a business blindly; knowing your direction is fundamental.

In my experience as a business owner, I've observed that many aspiring entrepreneurs lack clarity about the type of business they want to pursue. The challenge isn't a shortage of finances or viable opportunities; rather, it's about recognizing and seizing those opportunities.
If you can keenly observe your surroundings, you will uncover numerous untapped prospects. Consider our fundamental human needs: food, shelter, money, and more. Meeting these needs

presents lucrative business prospects.

While secondary needs like status or leisure also offer opportunities, focusing on primary needs often yields greater returns. As we said in the beginning, starting a new business may seem daunting, but generating ideas isn't the real challenge; it's executing them effectively.

Every thriving business began as someone's inspiration, but the journey from idea to success is arduous. The process demands time, effort, and financial investment. As Thomas Edison famously stated, genius is "1 percent inspiration and 99 percent perspiration." This sentiment rings true in the business world.

A good idea is just the start; the real test lies in its execution. Thus, the goal is not only to conceive a great idea but also to implement it successfully. That's the true mark of entrepreneurial success.

So, what's the best type of business to start?

Focus on fulfilling a market need. Your mantra should be: "Find a need, fill it." Businesses that address genuine needs tend to thrive. If you're seeking a business idea, prioritize finding something that meets a customer need.

Exploring Diverse Opportunities

Embarking on the journey of finding a lucrative business idea can initially feel daunting if you don't have a eureka moment right from the start. It seems like every avenue has already been explored, leaving you wondering where to even begin.

But fear not! Amidst this sea of choices lies the key: recognizing the myriad opportunities that exist. Let's start by outlining seven types of opportunities, and then we will delve deeper into each:

- Look for a deficiency in the original product.
- Identify and solve a customer pain point.
- Cater to consumer passions.
- Build an intriguing and captivating brand.
- Capitalize on trends early.
- Leverage your own experience and expertise.
- Follow your passion.

Each opportunity entails a unique mindset and approach. Let's unpack them further:

1. **Look for a deficiency in an existing product**: Research, Research, Research, and More Research: Your initial step involves delving deep into the marketplace and exploring the array of opportunities available. Scan the market for existing products with room for improvement or unaddressed needs. This gap might manifest as a missing feature or an untapped market. Look for a business that not only captures your attention but also exhibits potential for growth and aligns with your interests. Assess the feasibility of starting a similar venture: How challenging is it to establish? What is the potential revenue? How much initial investment is required? Thankfully, there's no shortage of resources to guide you through this process.

2. **Identify and solve a consumer problem:** One of the most effective strategies for building a robust business is tackling consumer pain points head-on. By providing solutions to these challenges, you not only meet a demand but also cultivate consumer loyalty. Remember, these pain points can range from practical inconveniences to emotional frustrations.

3. **Cater to consumer passions**: Consumers are willing to invest in products or services that align with their interests and hobbies. By tapping into these passions, you can foster deeper brand engagement and cultivate a loyal customer base.

4. **Build an interesting and captivating brand**: Distinguish yourself from competitors by crafting a compelling brand identity. This involves understanding your target audience, crafting a unique brand story, and carving out a distinct niche in the market. A strong brand not only attracts customers but also fosters brand loyalty amidst stiff competition.

5. **Capitalize on market trends:** Stay ahead of the curve by identifying emerging market trends and seizing them early. Doing so not only positions your brand as an industry leader but also establishes a strong foothold in consumers' minds before competitors catch on.

6. **Leverage your own experience and expertise**: Consider your professional background and expertise. For instance, if you've honed your skills in marketing, leverage that knowledge when selecting your business venture. While you might be inclined to pursue a new direction, it's wise to capitalize on your existing competencies. Your unique background and skills can serve as a valuable competitive advantage.

7. **Follow your passion:** Building a business around your passions instills the resilience needed to navigate challenges. However, don't shy away from creativity. Harness your creative thinking skills to innovate and breathe new life into your business endeavors.

Additionally, consider identifying business opportunities based on your own special needs or those of others around you. Embarking on the journey of finding a lucrative business idea is challenging, therefore:

- Exercise patience. Identifying the right business idea

demands time and a deep understanding of the industry, marketplace, and competition.

- Don't bite off more than you can chew with an overly challenging business. Remember, there will be plenty of challenges along the way.
- Don't venture into a business arena where you can't compete. Instead, carve out a niche where you can outshine the competition.

Armed with this knowledge, you're well-equipped to generate a robust list of potential product ideas worth exploring further.

CHAPTER 6: Growing Your Business

If expanding your business is your goal, now is the perfect time to devise a concrete action plan. Relying on vague, scattered ideas won't bring you closer to your goals. What you need is a well-thought-out strategy for growth, one that follows a clear path.

With a growth strategy in place, you'll have a roadmap that shows exactly where your business is headed and how to reach those milestones. Let's get started on this journey towards success!

Why Did You Start Your Business In The First Place?

So, let's dive into why you started your business in the first place. Remember that initial spark, that vision you had? It's essential to revisit it now and then to make sure it still resonates with you and your lifestyle. One way to keep that vision alive is by finding a visual representation that reminds you why you're in this game.

It could be an uplifting quote, a motivating picture, or anything else that speaks to your entrepreneurial spirit. Keep it somewhere visible, where you can see it every day, to reignite that passion and purpose.

Now, let's talk about why you want to grow your business at this moment. For many, it's about making more money, which is totally valid. But for others, it could be about working less, reducing stress, preparing for retirement, or having the freedom to travel more.

Whatever your reasons, it's crucial to get clear about where you want to go. This clarity forms the foundation of your business mission. It's like your guiding star, steering you towards your goals and keeping you focused on what truly matters.

So, take some time to reflect on your why, and let it fuel your journey towards growth and success! Next, lets see ways

Growing Your Business

To foster growth in your business, let's explore some ideas on how you can achieve it by implementing the following strategies:

- **Find more customers:** This could involve ramping up your marketing efforts, reaching out to new demographics, or exploring untapped markets.
- **Increase your prices:** Sometimes, a strategic price adjustment can not only boost revenue but also enhance perceived value.
- **Encourage existing customers to buy more**: Implement loyalty programs, cross-selling tactics, or exclusive offers to incentivize repeat purchases.
- **Enter new markets:** Expansion into different geographical areas or diversifying your product/ service offerings can open up fresh opportunities.

You can decide what kind of growth aligns best with your vision. If you're ready to dive headfirst into rapid expansion, fast and furious approach might be for you. It requires bold moves and quick decisions.

Alternatively, if you prefer a more measured approach, focusing on steady, sustainable growth might be the way to go. It allows for careful planning and gradual progress. Organic growth, though it takes longer, can yield the most enduring results.

It's like nurturing a plant from seed to fruit-bearing tree—it may take time, but the rewards are plentiful and lasting. Now, paint a vivid picture of where you envision your business in the next 6 months.

Building Your Ideal Customer Profile

Targeting the right audience is a crucial step in your marketing strategy. Many of us tend to cast a wide net when it comes to marketing, hoping to appeal to everyone under the sun. But here's the truth: when you try to speak to everyone, you often end up speaking to no one in particular.

If you're not connecting with the right audience, it doesn't matter how fantastic your product or service is – you're just not going to make those sales. Instead, you want to focus your efforts on identifying your primary target audience – those people who are the best fit for what you're offering.

So, who exactly do you want to serve? And just as importantly, who do you NOT want to work with?

It's crucial to be crystal clear about this. You want to hone in on the specific individuals who are most likely to buy from you and benefit from what you have to offer.

Now, let's talk about the benefits. What problem does your primary product or service solve?
Understanding this is vital to crafting your message and resonating with your audience. Your goal is to show your potential customers exactly how your offering can make their lives better.

If you're new to the business world, don't worry – you're laying the groundwork now for future success. And if you already have customers, use the data from past sales to help refine your targeting and messaging. It's all about connecting with the right people in the right way.

Here are some essential facts to help you form a clear picture of your Ideal Customer Profile (ICP).

1. **Demographics**
   - Demographic details encompass:
   - Age, Location, Gender
   - Income, Education, Marital status

Each of these factors plays a role in shaping your marketing strategies. To gather this info, you'll want to ask simple, straightforward questions like:
   - How old are you?
   - Where do you live?
   - What's your annual income?

2. **Psychographics**

Psychographics provide a window into the inner workings of your customer's mind, showcasing their interests, attitudes, and personality traits. This includes everything from their individual values and hobbies to their broader lifestyle choices and general behavior.

Your aim is to gain a holistic understanding of the personality traits that make up your Ideal Customer Profile (ICP). Understanding these nuances will pave the way for tailored strategies that resonate deeply with your target audience.

3. **Behavioral Characteristics**

Knowledge of the behavioral traits of your target audience is essential for developing effective marketing tactics. Let's examine two crucial characteristics:
   ➤ Social Media Habits

When you pinpoint your ideal customer on social media, ask

yourself:
- Where do they hang out?
- When do they frequent these platforms?
- How much time do they spend there?

This insight helps tailor your marketing channels and choose the right platforms to establish a presence. Utilize social media analytics to deepen your understanding of your customer base. Consider these questions:
- Is your ideal customer active on social media? While most are, avoid assumptions without verification.
- Which platforms do they prefer?
- What purposes do they use social media for? Personal, professional, or both?
- How often and at what times do they engage on these platforms?
- How do they interact with content and which groups do they participate in?

> **Buying Behaviors**

Knowing your customer's purchasing habits guides your marketing approach. Understand why they buy and their sentiments towards consumerism, pricing, and buying patterns. Answer these critical questions:
- Do they make impulsive purchases or deliberate decisions?
- Are they price-sensitive or prioritize quality and status?
- Are they repeat buyers or one-time purchasers?
- Do they prefer online or in-person shopping?
- Are they inclined to watch product demos before purchasing?
- Do they prefer a trial before committing?
- How much research do they conduct before

buying?
- Do they rely on social proof for their decisions?
- How frequently do they make purchases?
- What's their average monthly spending on your product or service?

Harnessing the Power of Your Ideal Customer Profile (ICP)

Now that you've got your ICP nailed down, it's time to put it into action immediately. Your ICP isn't just a document to file away—it's a dynamic tool that can turbocharge your business growth in numerous ways:
- Building your community
- Attracting new leads
- Branding your business
- Content creation
- Sales and marketing
- Onboarding new team members

Now, the big question is: Where should you focus your efforts to leverage your detailed ICP for the greatest impact at this moment? Here are some ideas to consider:
- Use your ICP to enhance your current sales copy
- Utilize it to refine and develop your products and services
- Incorporate it into your marketing strategy
- Implement it during the onboarding process for new employees, and ensure that all team members involved in sales and marketing are well-informed.

To excel in your marketing efforts, it's crucial to recognize the significance of your Ideal Customer Profile (ICP). This involves identifying the purchasing behaviors and preferences that shape the most effective marketing tactics for reaching your target audience.

Take a deep dive into your available data to pinpoint how various elements influence your marketing decisions. By analyzing this information, you'll gain valuable insights into which strategies align best with your ICP.

Your ICP serves as a compass, directing you towards the marketing tactics that are most likely to resonate with your audience.

What Is Your Financial Situation

Whatever motivates your desire for growth, knowing where your company is financially today is critical. So, make sure you understand your profit sources. Consider your current offers, including both products and services:

What are the prices for each?
What is the cost of delivering them?
Most importantly, what is the profit margin for each?

Gathering this critical information now prepares the groundwork for your business growth plan later on. Having this information on hand will be a game changer as you plot your course to success.

Analyse Your Strength

Let's look at the S.W.O.T. Model, which is an excellent tool for assessing your company's current state and identifying the variables that are driving and impeding growth.

Consider this: the model is divided into four quadrants: strengths, weaknesses, opportunities, and threats. Each quadrant provides vital insights about your company's landscape.

But remember, while we'll look at each quadrant independently, it's important to keep the broader picture in mind because they frequently overlap.

First, what are your strengths? These are the things that differentiate you from the competition and give your company its distinct edge. Take a moment to determine what sets you apart.

Think about what you truly love doing. Passion drives success! Consider what your organization excels at. What makes you different? Consider where you bring exceptional value, perhaps through your years of experience.

Recognize where you stand out, maybe because of your expert knowledge or specialized skills. By acknowledging and leveraging your strengths, you're laying a solid foundation for your business growth journey. Keep these in mind as we navigate through the rest of the S.W.O.T. analysis.

Highlighting Your strengths

These are the gems that will truly set you apart: You've built a solid base of repeat consumers who trust and rely on your products/services. Your business thrives on positive word-of-mouth recommendations, which says volumes about the value you provide.
With your significant knowledge and skill, you've established yourself as the go-to person in your business, providing people with high-quality solutions.

Now take a time to reflect on your journey thus far. Consider the milestones you've reached and the triumphs you've celebrated. These can help you identify even more of your skills and assets, laying the groundwork for future growth and success.

Accepting Your Weakness

Weaknesses in your business are the areas where your business might not be as strong as it could be. For instance: Maybe you haven't yet developed a strategic marketing plan. Or perhaps you're not gathering valuable customer insights.

But don't beat yourself up about these weaknesses. In business, as in life, there's always room for improvement. You probably have aspects of your business that you're itching to change, right? And as your business grows, it'll naturally shine a light on any weaknesses you have.

Instead of dwelling on them, try to envision the future potential behind these weaknesses. Address them head-on now, and you'll only make your business stronger down the road. It's all about recognizing where your business might be struggling. But remember, every weakness is just an opportunity for growth and improvement.

Questions to ask yourself:
- What's holding you back from growth? Reflect on any obstacles hindering your business's progress.
- What resources do you lack? Identify any essential tools or support you're currently missing.
- Which parts of your business are not very profitable? Pinpoint areas where you're not seeing the returns you expected.
- Where do you need further education and/or experience? Consider areas where additional knowledge or expertise could benefit your business.
- What are your biggest time drains? Identify tasks or processes consuming significant time and energy.

Going Forward:
- Highlight areas of underperformance, like customer service or sales follow-ups.
- Identify offers or initiatives that aren't yielding results and consider eliminating them.
- Determine where additional experience or training is necessary.
- Assess areas where cost-cutting measures could be implemented.
- Evaluate staffing levels and consider adjustments where necessary.

By addressing these questions and taking action based on the insights gained, you'll be well-equipped to propel your business towards greater success.

Discovering Untapped Opportunities

Here are some questions that may help you discover hidden opportunities to help you achieve your goals:

- How can you do more with your existing customers or clients?

Think about ways to deepen your relationships with your current customer base. Are there additional products or services you could offer them? Could you enhance your customer service to improve their experience and encourage repeat business?

- What new target audiences do you have the potential to reach?

Explore potential customer segments that you haven't tapped into yet. Consider demographics or market niches that align with your offerings but haven't been targeted effectively.

- Do you have projects on the side-burner that you've been putting off which could add revenue?

Take a look at those projects you've been procrastinating on. Could any of them be turned into revenue-generating opportunities? Sometimes, the ideas we've shelved hold great potential.

- Do you or your team have talents, skills, or experience that you aren't using?

Assess the skills and expertise within your team. Are there any hidden talents or abilities that could be leveraged to benefit your business? It's worth exploring how you can make the most of the resources you already have.

- How can you use new technology to enhance your business?

Stay ahead of the curve by incorporating the latest technological advancements into your operations. Whether it's streamlining processes, improving communication, or enhancing your product/service offerings, technology can be a game-changer.

- What partnerships in related areas of products and services could provide an opportunity for your business?

Explore potential collaborations with businesses in complementary fields. Partnering with others can open up new avenues for growth and expansion that you may not have considered on your own.

- Are there any external forces that could help your business?

Keep an eye out for external factors or trends that could positively impact your business. This could include changes in regulations, shifts in consumer behavior, or emerging market opportunities. Remember, the path to success is often paved with strategic thinking and proactive decision-making!

Competitor Research Questions

By thoroughly analyzing these aspects of your competitor's business, you'll gain valuable insights to inform your own strategies and stay competitive in the market. For each of your main competitors, you'll want to tackle the following questions:
- Who are they? Provide a brief overview of who your competitor is and what they offer.
- What are their strengths? Identify areas where they

excel or have a competitive advantage.
- What are their weaknesses? Pinpoint areas where they may be vulnerable or lacking.
- What opportunities do they present? Look for potential areas of growth or collaboration.
- What threats do they pose? Consider any challenges or risks they might pose to your business.

- Marketing Approach: How does your competitor reach out to its customers? Are they leveraging specific channels or platforms effectively?
- Pricing Strategy: What are the price points your competitor sets for its products or services? How do these compare to yours?
- Unique Value Proposition: What sets your competitor apart? Do they offer something unique or innovative that attracts customers?
- Innovation and Value Translation: How does your competitor innovate, and how does this innovation enhance the value they provide to customers?
- Company Size and Workforce: How big is your competitor in terms of employees? Are they a large corporation or a smaller enterprise?
- Employee Quality and Expertise: What is the caliber of your competitor's employees? Do they boast significant experience or notable credentials?
- Ownership: Who owns the business? Understanding the leadership behind your competitor can provide insights into their strategic direction.
- Media Presence: Where can you find your competitor in the media? Do they advertise on TV, maintain an active presence on social media, or utilize other channels?
- Online Presence and Engagement: What kind of web presence does your competitor have? How engaged are they with their customers online?

- Reputation: What is your competitor's reputation like? Consider online reviews, social media comments, and market research to gauge public perception.
- Distribution Channels: How does your competitor distribute or deliver its products or services? Are there any unique distribution methods they employ?
- Special Services: Does your competitor offer any special services or features to customers? How does this contribute to their value proposition?
- Financial Strength: If available, obtain a copy of your competitor's annual report to assess their financial resources.
- Customer Perception: What do your competitor's customers view as their strengths and weaknesses? Understanding customer sentiment can reveal areas for improvement.
- Customer Loyalty: How loyal are your competitor's customers? Look for signs of long-standing relationships or repeat business.
- Customer Trends: Have there been any recent changes in your competitor's customer base? Are they experiencing growth or decline?
- New Product Development: What new products or services is your competitor working on? This can indicate future areas of competition or expansion.
- Financial Resources: Assess the financial resources available to your competitor. This can influence their ability to invest in growth initiatives.

CHAPTER 7:
MARKETING MASTERY

In the nooks and crannies of our cities and towns lie seemingly ordinary businesses: dry cleaners, barbershops, restaurants, and the like. Yet, within these humble establishments lies the potential for extraordinary success. It may start with modest beginnings, but the key is to dream big.

If you stroll down the streets, you will notice small business owners idly waiting for customers to grace their shops with their presence. But it doesn't have to be this way. There are simple yet effective techniques these entrepreneurs could employ to draw in new customers and boost their sales, rather than simply waiting around.

These very techniques are what industry giants use to dominate the market. You can harness them to transform your ordinary-looking business into a revenue-generating powerhouse. Take the time to absorb each point and then dive straight into implementing them.

- Quality Assurance and Credibility:

Maintain high-quality standards for your products or services. Study comparable offerings in the market and aim to match or surpass their quality. Avoid sacrificing quality for short-term gains, as it may lead to repercussions. Present your offerings credibly to instill confidence in potential customers. Providing free samples can allow them to experience the quality firsthand, fostering trust in your brand.

- Fostering Mutual Benefits and Relationships

The success of your business heavily relies on the quality of service you offer. Strive to establish mutually beneficial relationships with your customers. Tailor your offerings to meet their needs and preferences, and actively seek feedback to continuously improve.

Embrace collaboration opportunities that expand reach and enhance offerings. Prioritize customer satisfaction and positive relationships as the foundation for sustained business success.

- Competitive Pricing

If your goal is to capture a wide market, consider offering competitive prices without compromising on quality. Instead of overly focusing on undercutting competitors, concentrate on meeting the demands of your customers.

Develop a strategic plan that defines your objectives, products, and target market, ensuring that your pricing and service delivery provide customers with value that surpasses their investment.

- Packaging, Presentation, and Uniqueness

The presentation of your product or service significantly influences its success. Even the most innovative idea may struggle if poorly packaged. For service-based businesses, financial success often hinges more on effective packaging and presentation than substantial financial resources.

With the right skills and appealing presentation, anyone can succeed in this lucrative sector. Ensure your product is user-friendly, prioritizing convenience for busy individuals.

- Learning, Innovation, and Adaptation

Learn from successful business models, adapting proven ideas to your venture. These ideas have been vetted and can offer valuable insights. While your product or service doesn't need to be entirely new, strive to offer it uniquely.

Enhance existing offerings or deliver services exceptionally to distinguish yourself in the market. Keep up with industry trends and developments to remain competitive. Invest in education and self-improvement to enhance your skills and knowledge.

Continuous learning is crucial for business success, enabling you to make informed decisions and navigate challenges effectively.

- Excellence in Team Building and Resource Management

Emulate successful companies by attracting top talent and resources. Encourage excellence among your employees and provide opportunities for growth and development. Invest in sales training to optimize marketing efforts and drive business growth. Manage your resources wisely, particularly finances.

Avoid impulsive spending and allocate resources judiciously to support business objectives. Ensure fair compensation for yourself and contributions from friends and relatives towards your business's success.

- Strategic Planning and Execution

Develop a robust business strategy centered on acquiring and retaining customers. Conduct thorough market research to understand industry dynamics and competitor activities. Focus your resources on activities that maximize market share and competitive advantage.

- Effective Brand Promotion and Visibility:

Promote your business actively and confidently. Utilize

technology to enhance visibility and level the playing field. Establish an online presence through a website and embrace e-commerce solutions to reach a broader audience.

Be proactive in marketing and promoting your business, recognizing the importance of consistent effort for success.

Conclusion & Next Steps

Efficiently covering every aspect of building a successful business in a single piece like this is no small feat, but we've made a concerted effort to address the key components. Think of this guidance as a comprehensive toolbox, filled with strategies distilled from the experiences of successful entrepreneurs.

While not every strategy may align perfectly with your business model, incorporating a diverse range of techniques can significantly enhance your efficiency and productivity right away. By putting these strategies into action, you'll find yourself completing tasks more swiftly and with greater precision.

This, in turn, will afford you ample time to direct your focus towards other critical aspects of your business. Remember, building a successful business isn't a one-off lesson—it's an ongoing journey of refining and enhancing your operations. Continuously assessing your work processes is key to identifying areas ripe for optimization.

Whether it's through delegation, automation, or outsourcing, always remain vigilant for opportunities to streamline your workflow. Additionally, stay abreast of new tools and technologies that can further amplify your productivity.
Ultimately, business success transcends mere skill mastery—it hinges on nurturing the right mindset for sustained, long-term success.

ABOUT THE AUTHOR

I am excited to share my insights with you on the journey of building a successful business. My name is Kingsley Eleweke and my passion for entrepreneurship was ignited at a young age.

I was always curious to understand what makes businesses thrive, and over the years, I have gained invaluable hands-on experience as a startup enthusiast and seasoned business strategist.

Throughout my journey, I have come to realize that business success is not just about the destination; it's about the journey and the lessons learned along the path. My mission is to empower fellow entrepreneurs like you with practical wisdom and actionable strategies to navigate the exciting yet complex world of business ownership.

I'm thrilled to embark on this journey together with you and to help you unlock your full potential as a business owner. Let's dream big, work hard, and make those entrepreneurial visions a reality!